POETRY OF ECONOMICS
POLITICS AND COMPASSION

PROFESSOR PATRICK PIETRONI

FRESCO BOOKS

CONTENTS

INTRODUCTION

The first six volumes of this series covered:

The framework of these short booklets is to allow the reader to have an introduction to the specific focus of the book which are accompanied by poems and images that help to add an aesthetic and emotional experience.

In this volume I tackle the poetry of economics and politics. I have chosen to use the metaphor of the Greek God, Atlas, as understood in early mythology, having to hold up the Earth (celestial globe) on his shoulders as punishment for being unhospitable to Perseus (son of Zeus).

GAIA

Let us imagine that our own Earth is held up not by Atlas, but by the two "Gods" of Economics and Politics. Let us pretend they are also Greek Gods, *Economicus* and *Politicus*. We shall explore how each of one of these gods has been involved in supporting our globe - how they have changed over time and how they have either collaborated or, indeed, fought each other for primacy of being the more important of the two.

I will then introduce a third Goddess from the Buddhist scriptures, Guan-yin, which is short for Guanshiyin, which means *"The one who perceives the sounds of the World"*. In short, I believe that without the influence of Guan-yin, who in Buddhist mythology is associated with compassion, our other two stalwart Gods, Politicus and Economicus will fail in their task of ensuring the Celestial Globe/Mother Earth, or World, as we know it will continue to exist.

In passing, it is worth remembering that the *Gaia Hypothesis*, first formulated by James Lovelock in the 1970s, proposed that the earth should be understood as a *"complex self-regulating system, in its own biosphere"*.[1] He names this hypothesis after the Greek Goddess, Gaia, who in Greek mythology personified the Earth. Let us now examine how our two Gods have attempted to support life as we know and understand it. It is important to appreciate the timeline below which reminds us just how short a time homo sapiens have existed on planet earth.

THE EVOLUTIONARY DEBATES

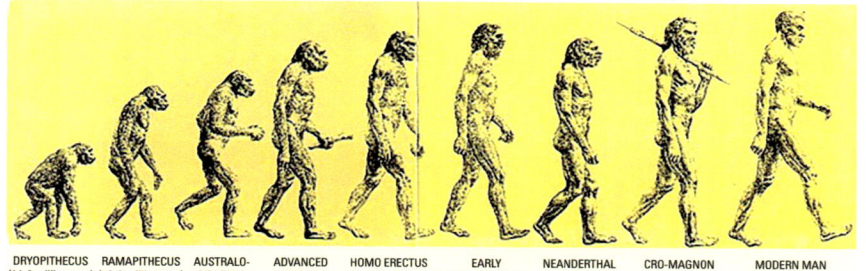

| DRYOPITHECUS (14-8 million yrs.) | RAMAPITHECUS (12-8 million yrs.) | AUSTRALO-PITHECUS (4 million yrs.) | ADVANCED AUSTRALO-PITHECUS (2 million yrs.) | HOMO ERECTUS (1.8-0.3 million yrs.) | EARLY HOMO SAPIENS (400,000-100,000 yrs.) | NEANDERTHAL MAN (150,000-30,000 yrs.) | CRO-MAGNON MAN 130,000-60,000 yrs.) | MODERN MAN (40,000 yrs. to present) |

OUR PRESENT TIME PERSPECTIVE

Big Bang (formation of universe)	1 January
Formation of Earth	14 September
Origin of life	25 September
Significant oxygen	1 December
First fish	19 December
First mammals	26 December
First humans	31 December
First cave painting	11:59 pm
Christ	11:59:56 pm
Renaissance	11:59:59 pm
Present day	First second of New Year's Day

The Gods of Economic Theory

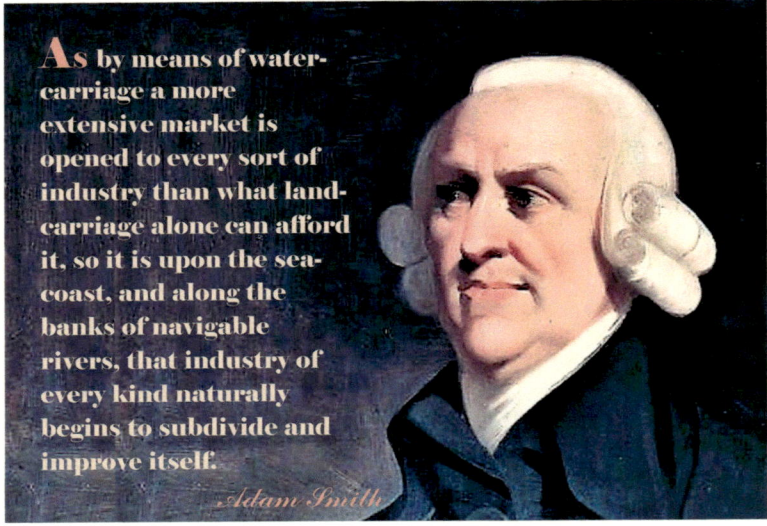

As by means of water-carriage a more extensive market is opened to every sort of industry than what land-carriage alone can afford it, so it is upon the sea-coast, and along the banks of navigable rivers, that industry of every kind naturally begins to subdivide and improve itself.

Adam Smith

Adam Smith (1723-1790)

Smith is seen as the "father of modern economic theory" and his two books, *The Theory of Moral Sentiments* [2] and *The Wealth of Nations* [3] are still viewed as the "bibles" from which others followed or challenged. His final post was as Rector of Glasgow University, and with his close friend, David Hulme, helped establish some of the economic policies that still exist to this day. His main beliefs included:

1. Bartering and bargaining are basic human beliefs and activities.
2. Exchange of goods or money benefits both parties.
3. 1 and 2 will lead to the division of labour (see below).

4. We act out of "self-interest" and this will lead to his famous phrase, *"We have the propensity to truck, barter and exchange one thing for another."*
5. This comes naturally to "human beings" and not to other animals. "Nobody saw a dog make fair and deliberate exchange of a bone with another dog." So it is this propensity, if encouraged, that will cause prosperity to increase. Government's role is to let it happen, not to direct it. [4]

He thus established what has been labelled as the "invisible hand" of economic theory, i.e. the Government's role is to let it happen and not try to control it.

Marx and Engels

Viewed the human species through the lens of groups, class, tribes or nations. Marx believed that the formation of social groups led to a succession of conflicts between "masters and slaves", lords and serfs, employers and employees, the bourgeois and the proletariat, and indeed, men and women. These conflicts existed because there was a disproportion between the ownership of property (capital) and industry (means of production). He wrote:

1. *The ruling ideas of each age have ever been the ideas of the ruling class.*
2. *The abolition of religion as the illusory happiness of the people is required for real happiness.* [5]

The Communist Manifesto (1848) [6] and Das Capital (1867) [7] essentially outlined the Marxist utopia which required, amongst other principles, the abolition of private property and ownership of factories. These principles are replaced by a top down, central

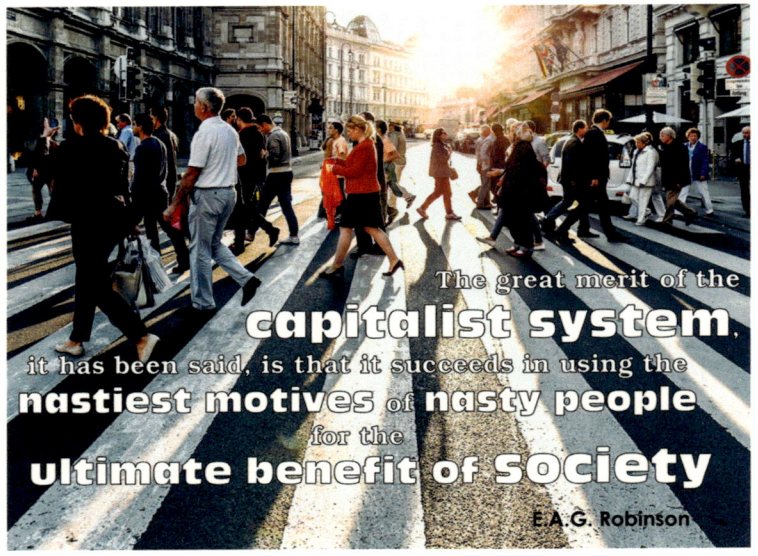

The great merit of the **capitalist system**, it has been said, is that it succeeds in using the **nastiest motives** of **nasty people** for the **ultimate benefit of society**

E.A.G. Robinson

control of the "means of production", i.e. the exact opposite to Adam Smith's free market and individual bartering model.

John Maynard Keynes (1883-1946)

Is considered to be the foremost economic theorist following the great depression of the 1930s. His book, *The General Theory of Employment, Interest and Money* (1936) [8] was often seen as a bible for world leaders for many years. He can be seen as trying to bring together the free market model (Adam Smith) and the central command and control model (Marx). His influence on governments only began to diminish in the 1980s with the return of the free market economics (von Hayek and Freidman – see below). Keynes believed governments had a responsibility to increase demand (public and private) by government spending.

He believed that encouraging consumer demand would boost growth and grow the economy. He believed that government spending on infrastructure (roads, transport, housing), together with investment in education and healthcare, would ensure the recovery from a depression. President Franklin D. Roosevelt followed Keynsian principles to establish the *New Deal Program* which rescued the US from the Depression of the 1930s.

Free Marketers (or the three Musketeers)
Friedrich August von Hayek, Ludwig von Mises and Milton Freidman

All three influenced both Ronald Reagan and Margaret Thatcher in the 1980s, and we saw a return of *laissez-faire* economics. All three in their separate ways were critical of Keynsian economics and would all sign up to the following statements:

> *Democratic socialism, the great utopia of the last few generations, is not only unachievable, but to strive for it produces something so utterly different that few of those who now wish it would be prepared to accept the consequences (von Hayek).* [9]

> *Those who were deeply concerned about the freedom and prosperity from the growth of government, from the triumph of the welfare state and Keynsian ideas were a small and beleaguered minority regarded as eccentrics by the great majority of our fellow intellectuals. (Freidman).* [10]

> *Free market commerce is the only system of human organisation yet devised where ordinary people are in charge, unlike Feudalism; communism; fascism; slavery and socialism.* [11]

Some Explanatory Stories

Economic theory can be somewhat complex, dry, and for some a little boring. Do remember though that the God Economicus is one of the two gods currently supporting life on this Earth. I list below a few "stories" that may make some of the previous section a little more understandable and human.

Tragedy of the Commons

Was first outlined by a British economist in 1833 and then popularised in an essay written by Garrett Hardin in 1968.[12] Elinor Ostrom wrote *Governing the Commons* [13] and won the Nobel Memorial Prize in Economic Sciences in 2009.

William Foster Lloyd [14] described what would inevitably occur if a group of cattle herders, or it could be sheep farmers, shared a plot of land, "the commons", for grazing their animals. If one farmer or herdsman put more animals to graze than he was entitled to, eventually the plot of land would become over-grazed. Only the one herdsman who had more of his share of land would have benefited. Some later commentators felt that the problem as described should be labelled, "The tragedy of the unregulated commons". This concept has now been applied to many other such situations:

Overfishing leading to the necessity for quotas
Forests and over logging affects climate change
Space exploration leading to debris in outer space
Uncontrolled birth rates leading to overpopulation

Modern critiques of the tragedy of the commons have argued:

> *The metaphor illustrates the argument that free access and unrestricted demand for a finite resource ultimately reduces the resource through over-exploitation, temporarily or permanently. This occurs because the benefits of exploitation accrue to individuals or groups, each of whom is motivated to maximize use of the resource to the point in which they become reliant on it, while the costs of the exploitation are borne by all those to whom the resource is available (which may be a wider class of individuals than those who are exploiting it). This, in turn, causes demand for the resource to increase, which causes the problem to snowball until the resource collapses (even if it retains a capacity to recover). The rate at which depletion of the resource is realised depends primarily on three factors: the number of users wanting to consume the common in question, the consumptive nature of their uses, and the relative robustness of the common.* [15]

It is interesting that the "Free-Marketers" use this argument to support "let the market decide" and "command and central control". Economists use the same argument for supporting the need not for "the invisible hand of the market", but for the very visible hand of the government.

Division of Labour

Our ancestors were forced to make and fashion all the food, shelter and tools that they needed for themselves. Once they met other groups and tribes, they could begin to barter and exchange food for tools or sheep for flour. Remember – money had as yet not been "invented". Bartering allowed each family and social grouping to reduce the need to produce goods they required to survive, and we saw the emergence of trades (carpentry, building, clothiers, ironmongery, etc.). As Adam Smith wrote,

The greatest improvement in the productive powers of labour seem to have been the effects of the division of labour.

And

Civilized society stands at all times in need of the co-operation and assistance of great multitudes. [16]

Thus bartering eventually led to the market where folk would meet to exchange goods. Once money was invented, there was no need for bartering.

THE RISE AND FALL OF MONEY

LOVE-MONEY AND US

A lady once wrote
"How do I love you?
Let me count the ways."

That was some time ago
And she never mentioned money.
Times have changed.
We are all captured by
Un-regulated market forces.
All is now commodified,
Categorised and sold.
All our transactions priced.

Does love now have a price?
Yes, of course it has,
But its value cannot be
Counted in Dollars/Pounds or Yen.

Your love appeared at the Lion Hotel.
Your eyes sparkled like diamonds,
Your voice was gentle and soft.
We soon found ourselves naked together,
And I delved into the treasures of your body.

But you are rich as well,
Richer than all the money you have,

Richer still because you share your riches.
Those who you give to
Only receive your money
And remain far poorer than I do,
For you give me what
Money can never buy.

No money could buy what you give,
And no money is needed to continue.
Our love is priceless and not for sale.
No shareholders need apply.
It will remain with us,
To enjoy and spend as we wish.

Anon [17]

Niall Ferguson's book, *The Ascent of Money* [18] charts the emergence of money – finance, monetary policy, the stock market and yes, the decent of money. I will quote some of the central passages from his book:

Money, it is conventional to argue, is a medium of exchange, which has the advantage of eliminating inefficiencies of barter; a unit of account, which facilitates valuation and calculation; and a store of value, which allows economic transactions to be conducted over long periods as well as geographical distances. To perform all these functions optimally, money has to be available, affordable, durable, fungible, portable and reliable. Because they fulfil most of these criteria, metals such as gold, silver and bronze were for millennia regarded as the ideal monetary raw material. The earliest known coins date back as long ago as 600 BC and were found by archaeologists in the Temple of Artemis at Ephesus (near Izmir in modern-day Turkey). These ovular Lydian coins, which were made of the gold-silver alloy known as electrum and bore the image of a lion's head were he forerunners of the Athenian tetradrachm, a standardized silver coin with the head of the goddess Athena on one side and an owl (associated with her for its supposed wisdom) on the obverse. By Roman times, coins were produced in there different metals: the aureus (gold), the denarius (silver) and the sestertius (bronze), ranked in that order according to the relative scarcity of the metals in question, but all bearing the head of the reigning emperor on one side, and the legendary figures of Romulus and Remus on the other. Coins were not unique to the ancient Mediterranean, but they clearly arose there first. It was not until 221 BC that a standardized bronze coin was introduced to China by the 'first Emperor', Qin Shihuangdi. In each case, coins made of precious metal were associated with powerful sovereigns who monopolized the minting of money so as to exploit it as a source of revenue. [19]

The invention of money ensured that the "human relational" quality of bartering was replaced by the anonymous, transactional quality and the invention of the market: stock exchange, bonds, derivatives, bear/bull markets, leverage, securities banks clearing houses The Federal Reserve boom and bust liquidity crises and the bit coin. And of course the Lehman Brothers bankruptcy and the 2008 crash which nearly caused Governments to fall, unemployment to rise and income inequality between the rich and the poor to become morally unacceptable.

Those arguing for what has been labelled as "creative destruction" will point out:

There is no longer much doubt that free commerce has a better economic or humanitarian record than command-and-control government. The examples just keep rolling in. Take the history of Sweden, for instance. Contrary to conventional wisdom, Sweden did not become wealthy as a result of having a big government imposing social democracy. When it liberalized a feudal economy and strongly embraced Smithian free trade and free markets in the 1860s, the result was rapid growth and the spawning of great enterprises over the next fifty years, new products). When it expanded government hugely in the 1970s, the result was currency devaluation, stag nation and slow growth, culminating in a full-blown economic crisis in 1992 and a rapid fall in the country's relative standing in the world's economic league table. When

*it cut taxes, privatised education and liberalised private
healthcare in the 2000s, it rediscovered growth.*

*Prosperity emerged despite, not because of, human policy. It
developed inexorably out of the inter action of people by a
form of selective progress very similar to evolution. Above all,
it was a decentralized phenomenon, achieved by millions of
individual decisions, mostly in spite of the actions of rulers.* [20]

Commentary on the above position is explored in depth in Philip
Roscoe's book, "I spend therefore I am: the true cost of economics",
and he states:

Selfish competition is the essence of economic theory. [21]

It is helpful to remember in this overview of economic theory
that Adam Smith, often labelled as the "God Father" of economic
theory, entitled his first book *The Theory of Moral Sentiment* [22]
and John Maynard Keynes, who is considered to be the most
important economist of the modern world, was heavily influenced
by John Stuart Mill who conceived of and founded the concept
of utilitarianism – *The greatest good for the greatest number.* [23]

So, what is emerging in this overview of economic theory is the
division between those who attempt to include "moral sentiments"
and those who conceive "selfish competition" as the basis of a
prosperous economy. We finish this section of this volume with
two more explanatory stories.

THE HIGHWAYMAN

As a man lost in thoughts, walked past,
highwayman roared,
awakened by solid shout,
man replied, I'as lost in thoughts,
not a penny in the pocket,
nor a grain in the house.
family is waiting for some grains
for todays dinner.
Is it so? let me see?
highway man checked and let him go.
man made a request,
can you lend me a penny?
smiling, and the highwayman replied,
this is twenty first century man,
taking risk is at a cost, for gains.
I could've killed you,
I didn't, risk outweigh gain,
charity is no risk, no gain,
go home, you'll get used to hunger,
or I'll make you my apprentice,
get trained in this art,
I'm expanding my venture
If so sign here and take this penny.

Ramachandran Rajasekhar [24]

Trickle Down Theory

This theory is often referred to as supply-side economics, and became known as *Reagonomics*. Briefly, those supporting this theory believe that by lowering taxes, especially on the wealthy, more money will be released into the economy and it will eventually trickle-down to those at the "bottom of the heap" and raise their income as well. It was also known as the "horse and sparrow" theory – if you feed the horse enough oats some will pass through to the road for the sparrows. No wonder it is referred to as "supply-side economics". It sounds so much more persuasive.

Creative Destruction

Some economic theorists have linked the "evolution" of the economy to a Darwinian motif, often referring to the concept of "survival of the fittest". In fact, Darwin never wrote this now infamous phrase to describe his theory. His statements and theories emphasise the necessity of adaption – *to survive we need to learn to adapt.*

Matt Ridley writes in *The Evolution of Everything*,

> *Schumpeter saw 'creative destruction' as the key to economic progress, and the 'essential fact about capitalism'. For new firms and technologies to emerge, old ones had to die. There is a 'perennial gale of creative destruction'. Or, as Nassim Taleb puts it, for the economy to antifragile (strengthened by running risks), individual firms must be fragile. The restaurant business is robust and successful precisely because individual restaurants are vulnerable and short-lived. Taleb wishes that*

society honoured ruined entrepreneurs as richly as it honours fallen soldiers.

Schumpeter was explicitly biological in his reasoning, referring to economic change as a process of 'industrial mutation'. He saw that an economy is like an ecosystem, in which the struggle for existence causes businesses and produces to compete and to change. He also saw that without risk-taking entrepreneurs, this economic evolution would not happen. Schumpeter's evolutionary perspective has recently been extended by the entrepreneur Nick Hanauer and the economist Eric Beinhocker. They argue that markets, like ecosystems, work not because they are efficient, but because they are effective, because they provide solutions to problems that face customers (or organisms). And the beauty of commerce is that when it works it rewards people for solving other people's problems. It is 'best understood as an evolutionary system, constantly creating and trying out new solutions to problems in a similar way to how evolution works in nature. Some solutions are "fitter" than others. The fittest survive and propagate. The unfit die. [25]

On the contrary, Darwin's research suggests that humans have evolved to behave compassionately or, at least, that we have the capacity to do so. Recent discoveries in neuroscience and neural-imaging support this biological basis for compassion, but it was Darwin who originally argued that

[T]hose communities which contained the greatest number of the most sympathetic members would flourish best, and rear the greatest number of offspring. [26]

Modern Darwinism shows how humans are intimately related to all other organisms on our planet, a cognitive-emotional tonic for improved biophilia as well as kinder, more inclusive relationships between human beings. Humans derive a sense of meaning from performing costly prosocial, altruistic acts, and happiness from receiving such kindnesses from others. The brain has developed in a way that allows us to engage in complex indirect and time-delayed reciprocity. We can experience the positive emotions associated with compassionate action without being immediately repaid by the same individuals we help. These positive emotions breed happiness and more compassionate action.

> *Sympathy beyond the confines of man, that is, humanity to the lower animals, seems to be one of the latest moral acquisitions.... This virtue, one of the noblest with which man is endowed, seems to arise incidentally from our sympathies becoming more tender and more widely diffused, until they are extended to all sentient beings.* [27]

We thus have identified the ever-present debate as exemplified by the current pandemic Covid 19. Do we "preserve the economy or do we preserve life"? We shall return to this question once we have covered the second God we introduced at the beginning of this volume, *Politicus*.

THE GODS OF POLITICAL THEORY

In contrast to the Gods of Economics, we find the Gods of Political Theory to be far more abundant and span many more centuries. I shall focus on the gods from the 17th Century onwards but will start with a brief overview of the earlier gods that helped to establish the philosophy underpinning politics.

The Greek Originators – Plato/Aristotle, Socrates/Alexander

STRANGE TIMES ARE THESE IN WHICH WE LIVE WHEN OLD AND YOUNG ARE TAUGHT FALSEHOODS IN SCHOOL. AND THE PERSON THAT DARES TO TELL THE TRUTH IS CALLED AT ONCE A LUNATIC AND FOOL.

Plato

The word *polis* is Greek for *city*. It was Plato who first elaborated the purpose of government, and his book, *Republic* [29] sets the stage for what was to follow. The book reads as a series of conversations between Plato and Socrates, and his famous metaphor of the cave underpinned his view that Kings and Princes ruled the Cities. Human beings remain trapped in the cave (facing the wall, and only experiencing the World through the shadows cast on the wall from the cave's entrance). He thus established the rule by one man, rather than one man chosen by the populace. So there was no democracy yet, but rule of law yes, as determined by the King/Prince who could be supported by a national council and curators of law.

Aristotle disagreed with Plato's model but supported the idea that man was different from other animals and was a political animal; by that he meant man was equipped from birth with intelligence and moral qualities. It is important to remember that slaves were never to be granted citizenship and were considered slaves by nature. Plato, Socrates and Aristotle saw the city state (the Polis) as the bases for civilization. This fact could no longer be held when Alexander the Great conquered most of the Eastern Mediterranean and created a vast Empire. This new entity contained several Cities, States and Polis that by no means covered the large population which now lived in this vast Empire.

The Roman Empire followed and included most of the lands of the Greek Empire, most of Western Europe, as well as most of England.

Marcus Aurelius (121 AD-180 AD) was one of the five Good Emperors. The others were Antoninus Pius, Nerva, Trajan and Hadrian). Marcus was also known as the Philosopher Emperor and considered himself a Stoic, writing a diary which became known as *Meditations.* [30]

Cicero was of great influence on Marcus and we begin to see what would later become known as "moral sentiments" creep into the political "bible". Cicero wrote that the purpose of Government was to

Make human life better by our thoughts and efforts. [31]

Constantine converted to Christianity in 312 AD and it became the sole religion throughout the Holy Roman Empire. St. Augustine's *City of God* [32] written in 413 AD forms the beginning of how the Christian Church became the only acceptable spiritual authority and would determine both the structure (Divine Right of Kings) and the laws (Ten Commandments) that constituted the laws of government.

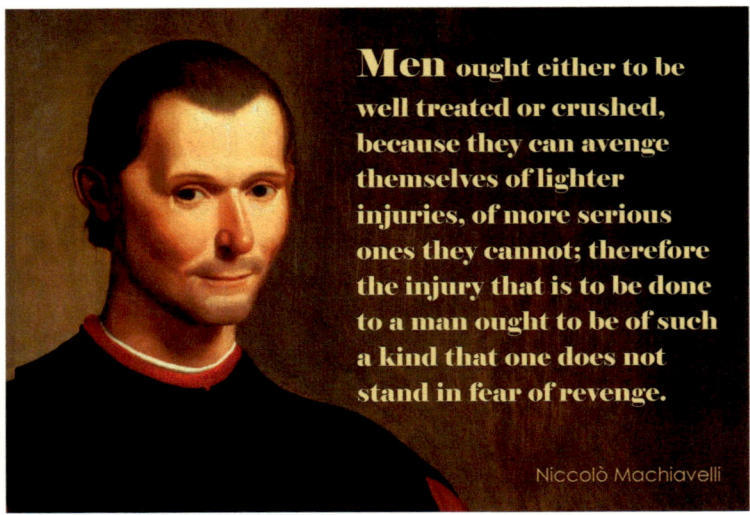

Men ought either to be well treated or crushed, because they can avenge themselves of lighter injuries, of more serious ones they cannot; therefore the injury that is to be done to a man ought to be of such a kind that one does not stand in fear of revenge.

Niccolò Machiavelli

The Pope in Rome and the Holy Roman Emperor were the dominant players for a few centuries. It was not until Machiavelli (1469-1527) wrote his famous book, *The Prince*, [33] that the secularisation of political philosophy could be said to begin.

His views of mankind were not that of a religious despot. He wrote,

> *Since the desire of men are insatiable, nature prompting them to desire all things and fortune permitting them to enjoy but few, there results a constant discontent in their minds, and a loathing of what they possess.*

He continues,

> *The Prince must combine the strength of the lion with the cunning of the fox. For men ought to be either well treated or crushed, because they can avenge themselves of lighter injuries, of more serious ones they cannot. Moreover, irresolute princes who follow a neutral path are generally ruined.* [34]

Machiavelli did believe in "the end justifies the means".

We can jump a century or two and begin to outline the emergence of modern political theory and ideology. These include:

Liberalism
Marxism
Socialism
Anarchism
Conservatism
Totalitarianism

The God Politicus had much to carry on his back as he held up Mother Earth.

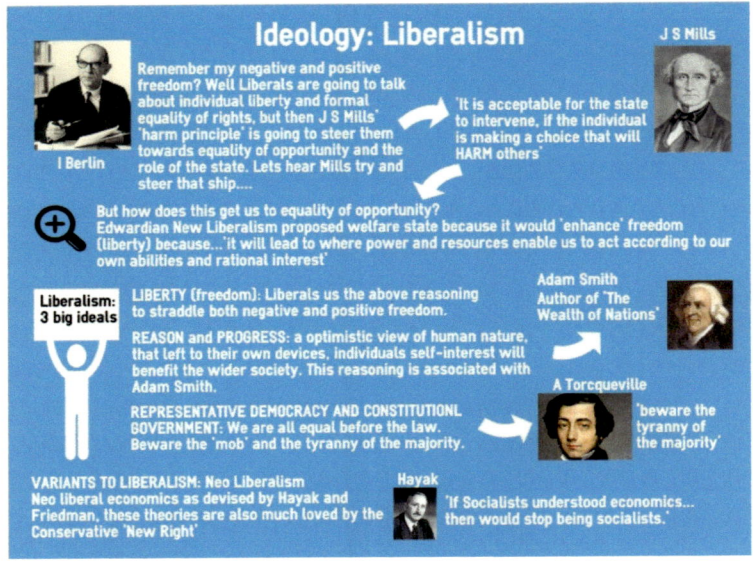

Ideology: Liberalism

I Berlin

J S Mills

Remember my negative and positive freedom? Well Liberals are going to talk about individual liberty and formal equality of rights, but then J S Mills' 'harm principle' is going to steer them towards equality of opportunity and the role of the state. Lets hear Mills try and steer that ship....

'It is acceptable for the state to intervene, if the individual is making a choice that will HARM others'

But how does this get us to equality of opportunity? Edwardian New Liberalism proposed welfare state because it would 'enhance' freedom (liberty) because...'it will lead to where power and resources enable us to act according to our own abilities and rational interest'

Liberalism: 3 big ideals

LIBERTY (freedom): Liberals us the above reasoning to straddle both negative and positive freedom.

REASON and PROGRESS: a optimistic view of human nature, that left to their own devices, individuals self-interest will benefit the wider society. This reasoning is associated with Adam Smith.

REPRESENTATIVE DEMOCRACY AND CONSTITUTIONL GOVERNMENT: We are all equal before the law. Beware the 'mob' and the tyranny of the majority.

Adam Smith
Author of 'The Wealth of Nations'

A Torcqueville
'beware the tyranny of the majority'

VARIANTS TO LIBERALISM: Neo Liberalism
Neo liberal economics as devised by Hayak and Friedman, these theories are also much loved by the Conservative 'New Right'

Hayak
'If Socialists understood economics... then would stop being socialists.'

Liberalism

From the word, *Liber* – being free. Liberalism has been the predominant political approach for the majority of European democracies and formed the foundation of the American Constitution. It is linked to the Age of Enlightenment.

> *By that time, Copernicus, the astronomer, had bravely published his life's work and put the sun at the centre of the universe, thus displacing the earth from its central position in the heavens. Galileo, who followed him, set about proving the brilliance of Copernicus' deductions, doing so with the aid of a giant telescope. So incensed were the elders of the Church of this 'blasphemous' behaviour that Galileo was arrested and under pressure,*

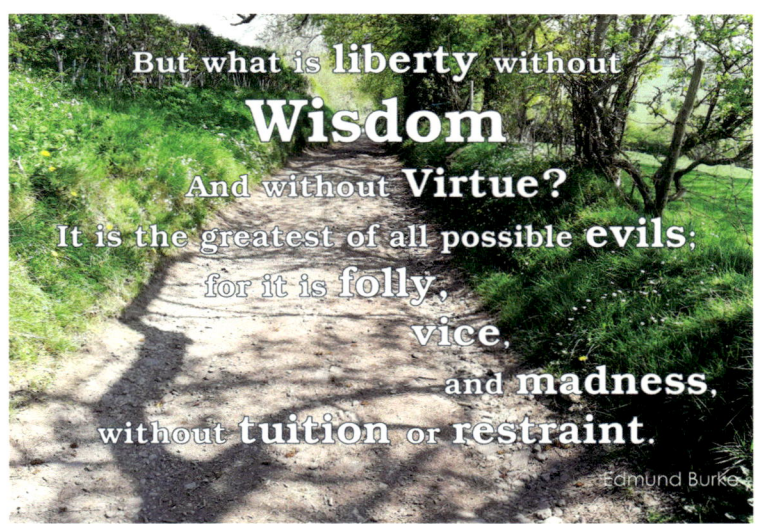

But what is **liberty** without **Wisdom** And without **Virtue?** It is the greatest of all possible **evils**; for it is **folly**, **vice**, and **madness**, without **tuition** or **restraint**.

Edmund Burke

recanted. The earth, however, did not return to the center of the heavens and this progress in understanding ourselves and our world was unstoppable. The separation of religion from science had begun and was firmly encouraged by two other great scientists, Isaac Newton and Rene Descartes. Newton's view of the universe was governed by reason – all events took place as a result of mathematical laws which were determined by the principle law of cause and effect. He pointed out that gods and spirits had nothing to do with why we developed disease. [35]

Thomas Hobbes, John Locke and Edmund Burke are seen as some of the first architects of this moral philosophy. In France, Montaigne, Rousseau and Voltaire emphasised the social, as opposed to the individual, aspects of liberalism. It was Jeremy

If socialists understood **economics**, they wouldn't be **socialists**

Friedrich von Hayek

Bentham who established the concept of Utilitarianism *(the greatest happiness for the greatest number)* and John Rawls who added the concept of fairness and justice in his book *Political Liberalism*. [36] Economics (Adam Smith) and the Free Market (Freidman von Hayek) all claimed the word "liberalism" as well. So Liberalism as a political concept can be seen as a coat hanger on which different ideas and functions are mixed in with different ideologies.

From the perspective of the focus of this volume (compassion), it is helpful to remember that the foundation stones of Liberalism included the issues of morals, ethics, fairness, justice and liberty.

Socialism

I find it helpful to view Socialism as a family of 'isms, including Marxism, Communism and Anarchism. More recently and starting in the Nordic countries the word Democratic is added to the word Social, as it was for a short period in the UK Social-Democratic Party (SDP). The word Socialism is derived from the Latin word *Socire* meaning to share. It was used to emphasise the opposite of the individualism which underpins the previous Liberalism and Capitalism.

Socialist theory emphasises that "it is the economic structure of society that helps to determine whether a society operates in an ethical, moral and just manner". It is the emphasis in sharing the collective economic framework that will allow for the four basic tenets as describe by Berki: [37] egalitarianism, moralism, rationalism and libertarianism.

Its roots in England go back to Levelers (post the revolution 17th Century) and also draws on the early Christian traditions which formed the basis of both the Methodist and Utilitarian movement. Liberation theology which arose in the Latin American Roman Catholic Church in the 1960s was based on socialist ideology. The Nordic countries adopted the term Democratic Socialism to emphasise the difference from the totalitarian models of Socialism which were present in both Marxism and Communism.

The following two quotations may help to put Socialism in historical context and in its relationship to Liberalism and Capitalism.

It really is impossible to understand either the French revolution or the early socialists unless one possesses some awareness

of the challenge which the new liberal individualism
represented to older ways of life. [38]

Socialism began a revolt against capitalism and its conception
of man and society was initially developed as an alternative
to the one which in the socialist view underlay and reinforced
capitalist society. [39]

Barbara Goodwin in her excellent short book *Using Political*
Ideas summarises the Nucleus of Socialism philosophy as follows:

The concern for poverty
A class analysis of society
Egalitarianism
Communal ownership for the means of production
Popular sovereignty
"Subordination of the individual to society"
Human creativity and sociability
The virtues of co-operation
Idealization of work as unalienated labour
Freedom as fulfilment
Internationalism [40]

SOCIALISM
VERSUS
DEMOCRATIC SOCIALISM

SOCIALISM	DEMOCRATIC SOCIALISM
Political and economic theory of social organization that advocates the means of production and exchange should be owned or regulated by the community	Democracy alongside social ownership of the means of production
Mainly focuses on the economic equality among the people	Mainly focuses on the economic and well as political equality, specifically in a democratic state
Advocates the public ownership of products	Does not advocate complete nationalization of properties

Critiques of Socialism all too often make the link with Marxism and Communism in order to underpin its totalitarian tendencies. In 1989 the 18th Congress of Socialist International adopted a new Declaration of Principles:

> *Democratic socialism is an international movement for freedom, social justice, and solidarity. Its goal is to achieve a peaceful world where these basic values can be enhanced and where each individual can live a meaningful life with the full development of his or her personality and talents, and with the guarantee of human and civil rights in a democratic framework of society.* [41]

Further changes to the concept of Socialism were introduced by Tony Blair, the Leader of the Labour Party in the UK in the 1990s. "The Third Way", as it was labelled stated:

> *The Labour Party is a democratic socialist party. It believes that, by the strength of our common endeavour we achieve more than we achieve alone, so as to create for each of us, the means to realise our true potential, and, for all of us a community in which power, wealth, and opportunity are in the hands of the many, not the few.* [42]

Conservatism

Embodies a commitment to an ideology and mentality rather than a focus on an outcome. Indeed, the outcome of a conservative ideology is very different in the UK than it is in Iran, for instance. So there can be, and there are, very different forms of Conservatism, e.g. Liberal Conservatism, Progressive Conservatism, Religious Conservatism and Authoritarian Conservatism. The tenets of this ideology emphasise tradition, continuity, hierarchy, authority and preservation of religious organisations. Conservatives will respond negatively to change and emphasise the importance of traditional, moral codes, social norms and property rights.

Edmund Burke (influenced by the horror of the French Revolution) is seen as the "father" of Conservatism as it developed in the UK and US. He wrote:

> *It is with infinite caution that any man ought to venture upon pulling down an edifice which has answered in any tolerable degree for ages the common purpose of society.* [43]

One of the important features of Conservatism is the belief in 'human imperfectability'. This leads to the support for strong, and at times authoritarian, government. The role of such governments is to uphold the law, to police the streets, punish the wicked and imprison the guilty. Such governments should protect rights of law abiding citizens and not interfere with the freedom of those who pursue their own destiny. This form of Liberal Conservatism is found both in the UK and the US. In the US the freedom to bear arms and defend one's property is considered a constitutional right.

The Thatcher Government in the UK encouraged the sale of "social housing" and adopted a laissez-faire economic policy that are the hallmarks of Capitalism (outlined in the next section).

Another important "pillar" of this form of Conservatism is the acceptance of the permanence of a hierarchical social system – "The poor will always be with us, or as Charles Dickens so elegantly wrote in *The Chimes*,

> *O let us love our occupations,*
> *Bless the squire and his relations,*
> *Live upon our daily rations,*
> *And always know our proper stations.* [44]

It is important to acknowledge that social hierarchical systems are found East/West and North/South. The most ingrained and widespread is in India (Hindu social organisation).

The strong desire for "no change" and stability leads to the centrality of national identity and the in-group/out-group phenomenon we have observed as a result of President Trump's

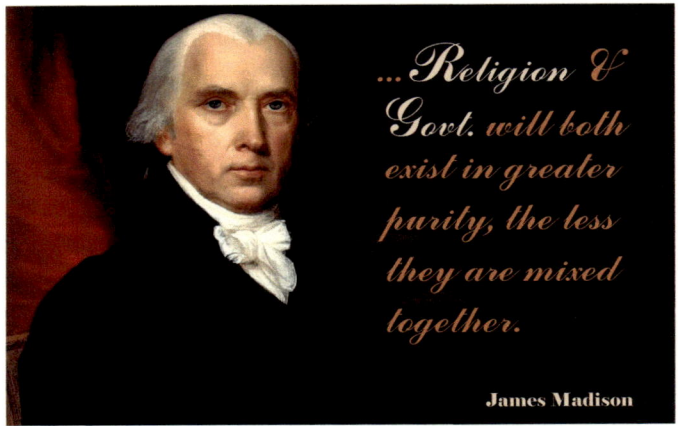

... *Religion & Govt. will both exist in greater purity, the less they are mixed together.*

James Madison

"Make America Great Again" (MAGA) which is not too distant from the desire to "Make America White Again".

The emphasis on individual freedom, individual responsibility, "small government" and low taxes leads to reducing the government involvement in the Welfare State and maximises individual philanthropy and charitable donations (from those who have to those who have not). The unintended consequence of this policy is to imbed the social hierarchy as a permanent feature in the country.

Conservatism and Capitalism are very closely linked, and we shall explore this further in the next section. I have not included in this short overview the other three models of political ideology (Marxism, Anarchism and Totalitarianism), as my own position is that compassion, which is the central theme of this book, is rarely, if never, found to exist in such systems of government. We will now explore how the introduction of compassion could/might influence the three models so far outlined – Liberalism, Socialism and Conservatism.

SUMMARY AND WHAT NEXT

WHAT DO THE THREE GODS AND GODDESSES HAVE TO OFFER TO MOTHER EARTH?

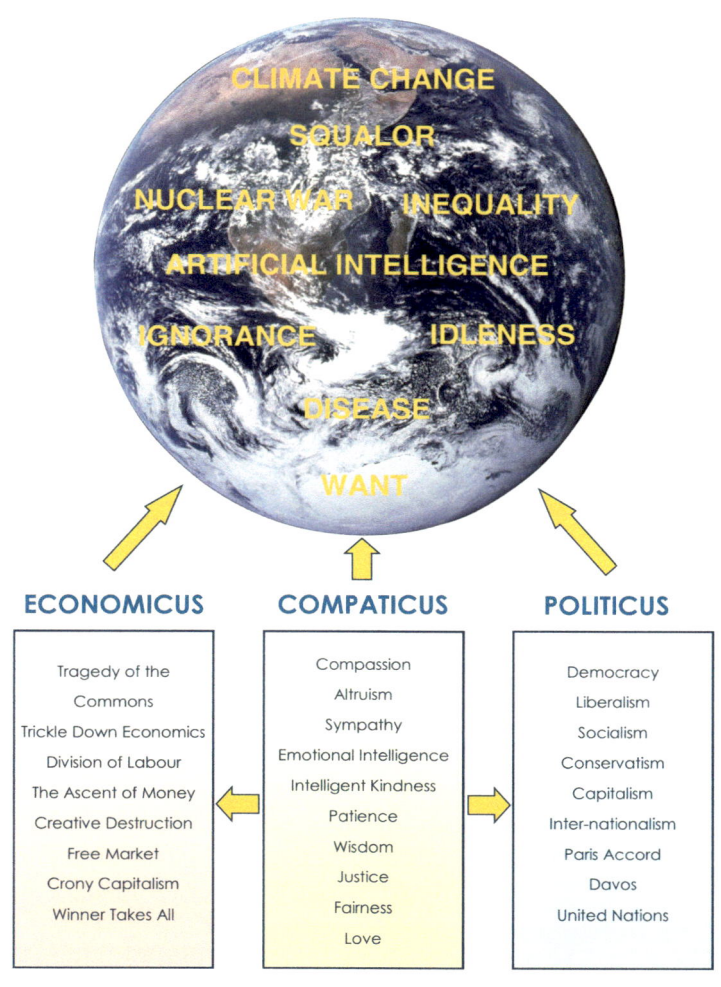

(Earth diagram labels: CLIMATE CHANGE, SQUALOR, NUCLEAR WAR, INEQUALITY, ARTIFICIAL INTELLIGENCE, IGNORANCE, IDLENESS, DISEASE, WANT)

ECONOMICUS

Tragedy of the Commons
Trickle Down Economics
Division of Labour
The Ascent of Money
Creative Destruction
Free Market
Crony Capitalism
Winner Takes All

COMPATICUS

Compassion
Altruism
Sympathy
Emotional Intelligence
Intelligent Kindness
Patience
Wisdom
Justice
Fairness
Love

POLITICUS

Democracy
Liberalism
Socialism
Conservatism
Capitalism
Inter-nationalism
Paris Accord
Davos
United Nations

In section one and two I have tried to summarise how the two pillars (Gods of Economics and Gods of Politics) have emerged. I outlined how they have been "holding up" the Globe – our Earth for the last twenty or so centuries.

Following the crash in 2008 and the current pandemic crisis we cannot avoid (even if we wanted to) that we are living through an existential crisis, and we have not even mentioned the issue of Climate Change.

This topic has not passed unnoticed by an avalanche of authors. I list below a small selection of those I chose to read in preparation for this short volume!

1. *And The Weak Suffer What They Must?*   Yaris Varoufakis [45]
2. *The State We're In*   Will Hutton [46]
3. *The Ascent Of Money*   Niall Ferguson [47]
4. *Post Capitalism: A Guide to our Future*   Paul Mason [48]
5. *The Crisis Of Global Capitalism:*   George Soros [49]
   Open Society Endangered
6. *The State We Need*   Michael Meacher [50]
7. *What Money Can't Buy*   Michael J Sandel [51]
8. *The Fourth Revolution*   Adrian Wooldridge
   John Micklethwait [52]
9. *The Body Economic: Why Austerity Kills*   David Stuckler
   Sanjay Basu [53]
10. *Progressive Capitalism: How to Achieve*   David Sainsbury [54]
    Economic Growth, Liberty & Social Justice
11. *Winners Take All: The Elite Charade of*   Anand Giridharadas [55]
    Changing the World
12. *I Spend Therefore I Am: How Economics*   Philip Roscoe [56]
    Has Changed the Way We Think & Feel

13. *Hope Without Optimism* Terry Eagleton [57]

To save you the task of reading this short selection, I add a list of the responses that are linked with these titles:

1. *Passionately sane, rich in ideas, breathes human sense back into economics and eloquently embodies the spirit of a new political optimism.*
2. *Open society endangered.*
3. *Europe, austerity and the threat to Global stability.*
4. *A guide to our future.*
5. *An exploration of what is meant to be human in an age of bewilderment.*
6. *Shrewdly anticipates the current financial crisis which has toppled banks, precipitated gigantic government bailouts and upended Global markets.*
7. *It is sure to spark many debates, and they are precisely the ones we should have.*
8. *The moral limits of markets.*
9. *This book is the best formula of the authentic religion that fits our dark time.*
10. *A brilliant and courageous book that no one who cares about the future of politics can afford to miss.*
11. *Why austerity kills.*
12. *How to achieve economic growth, liberty and social justice.*
13. *The elite charade of changing the World.*

Please feel free to try and attach these commentaries to the titles.

So, how can I in this final section try and summarise what these experts offer? I obviously cannot. What I can do is point out that in only one of these excellent texts does the word compassion appear in the references. So, yes, I have something to add.

Let us go back to the metaphor of Atlas holding up our Globe. We replaced him with the two Gods, Economicus and Politicus. We described how each of these two Gods had more than one "arrow in their quiver", or used a whole array of instruments to try to support the Earth. Some of these instruments included "moral sentiments", such as "the greatest happiness for the greatest number", or the importance of fairness and justice.

I would like to suggest that we now introduce the Goddess of Compassion with the words of the Dalai Lama, Charles Darwin and Wangari Maathai (2004 Nobel Peace Laureate):

Love and compassion are necessitates, not luxuries.
Without them, humanity cannot survive.
Dalia Lama XIV [58]

Sympathy beyond the confines of man, that is, humanity
to the lower animals, seems to be one of the latest moral
acquisitions.... This virtue, one of the noblest with which
man is endowed, seems to arise incidentally from our
sympathies becoming more tender and more widely
diffused, until they are extended to all sentient beings.
Charles Darwin [59]

In the course of history, there comes a time when humanity
is called to shift to a new level of consciousness, to reach a
higher moral ground. A time when we have to shed our
fear and give hope to each other. That time is now.
Wangari Maathai [60]

Before we introduce our Goddesses, let us try to identify what it is we would like them to address, i.e. what is it that the two

Gods, Economicus and Politicus, seem to have omitted from their responsibilities? It would be fair to say that there was mention of "moral sentiments" and the "greatest happiness for the greatest number", but no specific problems were identified, and no specific solutions were offered. We now must introduce to the Gods supporting the Globe the Five Giants that have been identified and require attention if the talk of moral sentiments, happiness and justice are not to be just words.

The Five Giants

The book *The Five Giants* written by Nicholas Timmins (Harper Collins 1995) is a biography of the emergence of the Welfare State in the United Kingdom. The Beveridge Report, [61] as it became to be known, was written at the instigation of the UK War Cabinet in 1942 and implemented by the Labour Government when it won the post-war election in 1945.

The Five Giants that Beveridge identified were: **Want, Disease, Ignorance, Squalor and Idleness.** I have selected some of the brief advisory notes sent to the Government on 25 June 1942.

Extract from notes from the advisory panel on Home Affairs on Reconstruction Problems: the Five Giants on the Road, 25 June 1942 (T 161/1165)

Assuming victory for the United Nations, is there any good reason for doubting our capacity after this war to do what was well within our reach just before it? We shall be poorer in the immediate aftermath of war, by loss of investments and in other ways. We shall not be able to afford so much waste or slackness. But need we, even in the immediate aftermath of war, be very much poorer than in 1936? And need we stay poorer for any length of time? Technical progress will not stop. To be afraid of the Giant Want is senseless cowardice.

Abolition of want in the sense in which that word is used here does not mean satisfying all desires. The extent to which the standard of living can be kept above the national minimum depends upon the degree of success achieved in dealing with the fifth giant: Idleness.

2. Disease: Attack on disease is a matter of prevention; second of cure. Prevention, beginning with health services in the narrow sense, spreads outwards into the problem of sanitation, housing, nutrition and local government. As to cure, opinion both public and professional, is probably ripe for a general re-organisation of the medical service of the community—so as to ensure that the best science of the community— so as to ensure that the best that science can do is available for the treatment of every citizen at home and in institutions, irrespective of his personal means. There are practical difficulties and sectional interests to be overcome in this field as in dealing with want, but no fundamental political issues.

3. Ignorance: Successful attack on Ignorance is a condition of good government under democracy. It is the only way of combining the efficiency of a dictatorship with the essential freedom of the citizen. Attack on Ignorance like attack on Want raises no fundamental political issues, and touches fewer vested interests. Progress on this line should be easy. But attack on Ignorance is not simply or mainly a question of raising the school age or widening the educational ladder tohigher schools and Universities. It is a question at least as much of adult education on an immense scale. That in turn means both getting more leisure and giving guidance in using leisure well.

4. Squalor: The irresistible disorderly growth of great cities, which may be described in one word as conurbation, is almost as great a social evil as unemployment. It has involved in the past daily waste of life and human energy in needless travel, bad housing and ill health, needless exhausting toil for the housewife in struggling with dirt and discomfort, habituation of the population to hideous surroundings. Co-urbation is a phenomenon as universal as unemployment- an inseparable accompaniment hitherto of private enterprise and private ownership of land. The only effective remedy is control of the distribution of industry, - control not persuasion, for population goes where industry calls for it. Distribution of industry in turn involves control of the use of land, imaginative central-ised direction of transport and public utilities, and re-organisation of local government. Here is a giant indeed.

5. Idleness: Want of the means subsistence could be abolished by a policy of the national minimum, as outlined above. But abolition of Want is an inadequate aim. Public opinion will demand that with income security shall go a reasonable oppor-tunity of productive work, not indeed with absolute continuity of jobs, but with more jobs than idleness for everyone. It will demand standards of living far above the minimum of physical subsistence. The policy of a national minimum must be combined with a policy of maintaining productive employment, of ensur-ing that the productive resources of the country are used to meet the needs of the people.

Next to the maintenance of peace, maintenance of productive employment is the most important of all reconstruction aims. It is the most important in itself; if the Giant of Idleness can be destroyed, all the aims of reconstruction come within reach.

CONCLUSION
The five giants are of an increasing order of strength and ferocity. Attacks on Want, Disease and Ignorance all affect sectional interests but raise no fundamental political issues. The task of framing these attacks is already to some extent in hand in regard to Want by the Inter-Departmental Committee on Social Insurance and Allied Services, in regard to Disease by the Ministry of Health and by that Committee, in regard to Ignorance by the Board of Education.

In regard to the two remaining giants the position is different. It is difficult to see how attacks on Squalor and Idleness could be pressed home by a Government which had not made up its mind for State planning, for some form of nationalisation of land or at least of land values, and for nationalisation of certain essential services. In other words attacks on Squalor and Idleness do raise what have been regarded as hitherto political issues. Whether they must continue to be so regarded, can be determined best by considering actual plans for maintaining productive employment and for distributing industry and population so as to prevent con-urbation and squalor. The making of such plans calls for the setting up of an Economic General Staff, which means neither a Committee of Ministers, nor a Committee of departmental officials, nor an Advisory panel, nor the Treasury or Board of Trade. It means, in fact, an Economic General Staff. It means an organ of Government which does not yet exist, with an access to the minds of decisive Ministers which has not yet been provided. [62]

If we were to embark on a Beveridge Report Mark II (2021), what would we now list as the Five Giants? The truth is we would need seven giants, because the first five discussed in the Beveridge Report are still the same. We need to address two new ones – Climate Change and Artificial Intelligence (some of these issues are addressed in Vol. III of this series of booklets – *The Poetry of Global Compassion*). So, let us introduce the Gods and Goddesses of Compassion. What do they offer to our two Gods, Economicus and Politicus?

In the first book of this series, I described how all the major world religions and humanistic organisations have identified "The Golden Rule" as the basis for compassionate thought, feeling and action (p.1-10, Vol. I). [63] I now supplement this list with the list of Goddesses linked to compassion and available to help both Economicus and Politicus. Looking back at Image 14 you will see what all these Goddesses can call upon in supporting Economicus and Politicus in their burdensome task. Remember the Dalai Lama's prayer:

Love and compassion are necessitates, not luxuries without them, humanity cannot survive. [64]

I finish with two poems one short and one long; the short one is written by myself and the long one written by Langston Hughes, that for me stands as a testament to where we have been, where we are, and where we should go with compassion.

COMPASSION AND THE OTHER

It is in the safety of
my own quiet corner
that I can acknowledge
my own shadow

Filled as it is with
all the blocks and hurdles
that limit my capacity
for compassion
to the other.
My shadow is my own other.

Know it
befriend it
you will find it
possible
to approach all the others
you will meet
on your own
journey
with compassion.

Patrick Pietroni [65]

LET AMERICA BE AMERICA AGAIN

Let America be America again.
Let it be the dream it used to be.
Let it be the pioneer on the plain
Seeking a home where he himself is free.

(America never was America to me.)

Let America be the dream the dreamers dreamed—
Let it be that great strong land of love
Where never kings connive nor tyrants scheme
That any man be crushed by one above.

(It never was America to me.)

O, let my land be a land where Liberty
Is crowned with no false patriotic wreath,
But opportunity is real, and life is free,
Equality is in the air we breathe.

(There's never been equality for me,
Nor freedom in this "homeland of the free.")

Say, who are you that mumbles in the dark?
And who are you that draws your veil across the stars?

I am the poor white, fooled and pushed apart,
I am the Negro bearing slavery's scars.
I am the red man driven from the land,

I am the immigrant clutching the hope I seek—
And finding only the same old stupid plan
Of dog eat dog, of mighty crush the weak.

I am the young man, full of strength and hope,
Tangled in that ancient endless chain
Of profit, power, gain, of grab the land!
Of grab the gold! Of grab the ways of satisfying need!
Of work the men! Of take the pay!
Of owning everything for one's own greed!

I am the farmer, bondsman to the soil.
I am the worker sold to the machine.
I am the Negro, servant to you all.
I am the people, humble, hungry, mean—
Hungry yet today despite the dream.
Beaten yet today—O, Pioneers!
I am the man who never got ahead,
The poorest worker bartered through the years.

Yet I'm the one who dreamt our basic dream
In the Old World while still a serf of kings,
Who dreamt a dream so strong, so brave, so true,
That even yet its mighty daring sings
In every brick and stone, in every furrow turned
That's made America the land it has become.
O, I'm the man who sailed those early seas
In search of what I meant to be my home—

For I'm the one who left dark Ireland's shore,
And Poland's plain, and England's grassy lea,
And torn from Black Africa's strand I came
To build a "homeland of the free."

The free?

Who said the free? Not me?
Surely not me? The millions on relief today?
The millions shot down when we strike?
The millions who have nothing for our pay?
For all the dreams we've dreamed
And all the songs we've sung
And all the hopes we've held
And all the flags we've hung,
The millions who have nothing for our pay—
Except the dream that's almost dead today.

O, let America be America again—
The land that never has been yet—
And yet must be—the land where every man is free.
The land that's mine—the poor man's, Indian's, Negro's, ME—
Who made America,
Whose sweat and blood, whose faith and pain,
Whose hand at the foundry, whose plow in the rain,
Must bring back our mighty dream again.

Sure, call me any ugly name you choose—
The steel of freedom does not stain.
From those who live like leeches on the people's lives,
We must take back our land again,
America!
O, yes,
I say it plain,
America never was America to me,
And yet I swear this oath—
America will be!

Out of the rack and ruin of our gangster death,
The rape and rot of graft, and stealth, and lies,
We, the people, must redeem
The land, the mines, the plants, the rivers.
The mountains and the endless plain—
All, all the stretch of these great green states—
And make America again!

Langston Hughes [66]

References

1. Tuney, J. (2003). *Lovelock and Gai.* London. UK Icon Books.
2. Smith, A. (2018. Originally published 1759). *The Theory of Moral Sentiments.* Digireads.com Publishing.
3. Smith, A. (1997. Originally published 1776). *The Wealth of Nations.* London. Penguin.
4. Goodwin, B. (1982). *Using Political Ideas.* London. John Wiley & Sons.
5. Marx, C. (1975. Originally published 1932). *Economic and Philosophic Manuscripts of 1844.* London. Penguin.
6. Marx, C., & Engels, F. (Originally published 1848). *The Communist Manifesto.* London. The Workers' Educational Association.
7. Marx, C. (2016. Originally published 1867). *Das Capital.* Delhi. Fingerprint! Publishing.
8. Keynes, J.M. (2018. Originally published 1936). *The General Theory of Employment, Interest and Money.* London. Palgrave Macmillan.
9. Von Hayek, F. (1967). *'The Principles of a Liberal Social Order' in his Studies in Philosophy, Politics and Economics.* London. Routledge & Kegan Paul.
10. Freedman, M. (1966). *Essays on Positive Economics.* Chicago. University of Chicago Press.
11. von Mises, L. (1922). *Socialism.* Alabama. The Ludwig von Mises Institute.
12. Hardin, G. (1968). The Tragedy of the Commons. *Science.* Vol.162, Issue 3859. pp.1243-1248.
13. Ostrom, E. (1990). *Governing the Commons.* Cambridge. Cambridge University Press.
14. Lloyd, W. F. (1833). *Two Lectures on the Checks to Population.* Oxford. S. Collingwood. Available at https://en.wikisource.org/wiki/

Two_Lectures_on_the_Checks_to_Population. Last accessed February 2021.

15. Brigham, D. (2007). Emerging Commons and Tragic Institutions. *Environmental Law*. 37:3. pp. 515-517. Available at https://www.jstor.org/ stable/43267404. Last accessed February 2021.

16. Smith, A. (1997. Originally published 1776). *ibid*.

17. Anon. (2020). *Love-Money and Us*. Unpublished.

18. Ferguson, N. (2008. First published 2007). *The Ascent of Money: A Financial History of the World*. London. Penguin Press.

19. Ferguson, N. (2008. First published 2007). *ibid*.

20. Ferguson, N. (2008. First published 2007). *op. cit.*

21. Roscoe, P. (2014). *I spend therefore I am: the true cost of economics*. London. Penguin.

22. Smith, A. (2018. Originally published 1759). *ibid*.

23. Keynes, J.M. (2018. Originally published 1936). *ibid*.

24. Rajasekhar, R. (2020). *The Highwayman*. Available at https://allpoetry.com/poems/about/Economics. Last accessed February 2021.

25. Ridley, M. (2015). *The Evolution of Everything: How New Ideas Emerge*. London. Fourth Estate.

26. Darwin, C. (1871). *The Descent of Man*, and *Selection in Relation to Sex*. London. John Murray.

27. Darwin, C. (1871). *ibid*.

28. Pietroni, P. (1990). *The Greening of Medicine*. London. Victor Gollancz.

29. Brown, E. (2017. First published 2003). Plato's Ethics and Politics in The Republic. *Stanford Encyclopedia of Philosophy*. Available at https://plato.stanford.edu/entries/plato-ethics-politics/. Last accessed February 2021.

30. Haines, C. R. (Ed.). (1930. First published 1916). *Marcus Aurelius*. Harvard. Loeb Classical Library. Available at https://www.loeb classics.com/view/LCL058/ 1916/pb_LCL058.v.xml. Last accessed February 2021.

31. Cicero, M. T. & Melmoth, W. (Trans.). (1889). *Old Age and Friendship.* Cassell's National Library no. 195.

32. Bettenson, H. Trans. (2003. First Published 1467). *St. Augustine - Concerning the City of God, Against the Pagans.* London. Penguin.

33. Machiavelli, N. (2010. First published 1532). *The Prince.* Glasgow. SoHo Books.

34. Machiavelli, N. (2010. First published 1532). *ibid.*

35. Pietroni, P. (1990). *ibid.*

36. Rawls, J. (1993). *Political Liberalism.* New York. Columbia University Press.

37. Berki, R. N. (1975). *Socialism.* London. J.M. Dent.

38. Lichtheim, G. (1969). *The Origins of Socialism.* London. Weidenfeld & Nicholson.

39. Parekh, B. (Ed). (1975). *The Concept of Socialism.* London. Croom Helm.

40. Goodwin, B. (1982. 2nd Ed). *Using Political Ideas.* London. Wiley & Sons.

41. Progressive Politics for a Fairer World. (2008). *Socialist International.* Available at https://www.socialistinternational.org/. Last accessed February 2021.

42. Labour Party Clause IV. (2008). Available at https://en.m.wikipedia.org/wiki/Clause_IV. Last accessed February 2021.

43. Goodwin, B. (1982. 2nd Ed). *ibid.*

44. Dickens, C. (1844). *The Chimes.* London. Chapman & Hall.

45. Varoufakis, Y. (2016). *And The Weak Suffer What They Must?* London. Penguin Random House.

46. Hutton, W. (1995). *The State We're In*. Random House.
47. Ferguson, N. (2009). *The Ascent of Money.* London. Penguin.
48. Mason, P. (2015). *Post Capitalism: A Guide to our Future.* London. Allen Lane.
49. Soros, G. (1998). *The Crisis of Global Capitalism: Open Society Endangered.* London. Little, Brown Book Group.
50. Meacher, M. (2013). *The State We Need.* London. Biteback Publishing.
51. Sandel, M. J. (2012). *What Money Can't Buy.* London. Penguin.
52. Woodlridge, A. & Micklethwait, J. (2014). *The Fourth Revolution.* London. Allen Lane.
53. Stuckler, D. & Baus, S. (2013). *The Body Economic: Why Austerity Kills.* London. Allen Lane.
54. Sainsbury, D. (2013). *Progressive Capitalism: How to Achieve Economic Growth, Liberty & Social Justice.* London. Biteback Publishing.
55. Giridharadas, A. (2018). *Winners Take All: The Elite Charade of Changing the World.* New York. Alfred A Knopf.
56. Roscoe, P. (2014). *I Spend Therefore I Am: How Economics Has Changed the Way We Think & Feel.* London. Viking Penguin.
57. Eagleton, T. (2015). *Hope Without Optimism.* London. Yale University Press.
58. Eckman, P. (2014). *Moving Toward Global Compassion.* London. Paul Eckman Group.
59. Darwin, C. (1871). *The Descent of Man*, and *Selection in Relation to Sex*. London. John Murray.
60. Maathai, W. (2004). Available at https://wangarimaathai.org/stories/my-little-thing/. Last accessed January 2021.
61. Timmins, N. (1995). *The Five Giants: A Biography of the Welfare State.* London. Harper Collins.

62. The National Archives. (1942). *Extract from notes from the advisory panel on Home Affairs on Reconstruction Problems: the Five Giants on the Road, 25 June 1942 (T 161/1165)*. Available at www.national-archives.gov.uk/ education/resources/attlees-.britain/five-giants/. Last accessed January 2021.

63. Pietroni, P. (2020). *The Poetry of Compassion*. Albuquerque. Fresco Books.

64. Eckman, P. (2014). *Moving Toward Global Compassion*. *ibid.*

65. Pietroni, P. (2020). *op.cit.*

66. Hughes, L. (1995). *Let America Be America Again*. Available at https://www.poetryfoundation.org/poems/147907/let-america-be-america-again. Last accessed February 2021.

Images

Image 1   Sculpture of Atlas. By ThreeOneFive (talk) - photograph, F/1.4
            1/320s, Public Domain, https://en.wikipedia.org/
            w/index.php?curid= 17300585. Page 5.

Image 2   Gaia. By Anselm Feuerbach - http://www.bildindex.de/
            obj19070503.html, Public Domain, https://commons.
            wikimedia.org/w/index.php?curid=9022191 Page 6.

Image 3   Evolutionary debates – image available at http://acerzam.
            blogspot.com/2016/09/evolution-of-human-stupidity.html.
            Page 7.

Image 4   Our present time perspective – adapted from Sagan, C. (1977).
            The Dragons of Eden: Speculations on the Evolution of Human
            Intelligence. New York. Radom House. Page 7.

Image 5   Adam Smith. Words: https://geolib.com/smith.adam/won1-03.html.
            Image by Unknown author - http://www.nationalgalleries.org/
            object/PG 1472, Public Domain, https://commons.wikimedia.org/
            w/index.php?curid=20413810. Design: DIISC. Page 8.

Image 6   Edward Austin Gossage Robinson. Words: https://quoteinves-
            tigator.com/2011/02/23/capitalism-motives/. Image: Jacek
            Dylag on Unsplash. Design: DIISC. Page 10.

Image 7   Plato. Words: https://www.goodreads.com/quotes/1140944-
            strange-times-are-these-in-which-we-live-when-old.
            Image: RaphaelQS - Own work, CC BY-SA 4.0,
            https://commons.wikimedia.org/w/index.php?curid=65546874.
            Design: DIISC. Page 24.

Image 8   Machiavelli. Words: https://pagebypagebooks.com/Nicolo_
            Machiavelli/The_Prince/CHAPTER_III_p2.html. Image:
            Santi di Tito - Cropped and enhanced from a book cover found
            on Google Images., Public Domain, https://commons.wikime-
            dia.org/w/index.php?curid=9578897. Design: DIISC. Page 26.

Image 9   Idelogy: Liberalism. https://learn1.open.ac.uk/mod/oublog/
viewpost.php?post=193007. Page 28.

Image 10 Edmund Burke. Words: https://quod.lib.umich.edu/
cgi/t/text/pageviewer-idx?cc=ecco;c=ecco;
idno=004795912.0001.002;node=004795912.0001.002:
12;seq=9;page=root;view=text. Image: Lee Good.
Design: DIISC. Page 29.

Image 11 Friedrich August von Hayek. Words: https://www.good
reads.com/author/quotes/670307.Friedrich_A_Hayek.
Image: Lee Good. Design: DIISC.   Page 30.

Image 12 Socialism versus Democratic Socialism.
https://pediaa.com/difference-between-socialism-and-
democratic-socialism/. Page 33.

Image 13 James Madison. Words: https://press-pubs.uchicago.edu/
founders/documents/amendI_religions66.html.
Image: https://commons.wikimedia.org/
w/index.php?curid=73110465 Design: DIISC. Page 36.

Image 14 What do the three Gods and Goddesses have to offer to
Mother Earth? Image: https://commons.wikimedia.org/
w/index.php?curid=636876. Design: DIISC. Page 37.

Image 15 Goddesses. Images:
https://commons.wikimedia.org/w/index.php?curid=6091994;
https://commons.wikimedia.org/w/index.php?curid=9944745;
https://greekgoddesses.fandom.com/wiki/Eleos?file=Eleos.jpg:
https://commons.wikimedia.org/w/index.php?curid=7146040;
https://commons.wikimedia.org/w/index.php?curid=1021683;
https://commons.wikimedia.org/w/index.php?curid=3005734;
https://buddhaweekly.com/guan-yin-ten-great-protections-
goddess-mercy-avalokiteshvara-bodhisattva-compassion/.
Design: DIISC. Page 46.

Publisher
SF Design, llc / Fresco Books
Albuquerque, New Mexico
frescobooks.com

ISBN: 978-1-934491-82-9